T0356073

MONICA BODIRSKY

SHADOWLAND
LENORMAND

REDFeather™
MIND | BODY | SPIRIT

4880 Lower Valley Road, Atglen, PA 19310

Library of Congress Control Number: 2020952567

Designed by Brenda McCallum
Type set in Amatic/Frutiger/Burning

ISBN: 978-0-7643-6240-8
Printed in China
5 4 3 2

Published by REDFeather Mind, Body, Spirit
An imprint of Schiffer Publishing, Ltd.
4880 Lower Valley Road, Atglen, PA 19310
Phone: (610) 593-1777; Fax: (610) 593-2002
E-mail: Info@redfeathermbs.com
Web: www.redfeathermbs.com

Other Schiffer Books by the Author:
Shadowland Tarot, ISBN 978-0-7643-5903-3

66

*I walked into
the shadows blindly
and returned with*

20-20 vision

99

This deck is dedicated to my
husband, partner, and best friend, Allan,
in shadows and light.

Acknowledgments

I gratefully acknowledge my ancestors, family, friends, and witch and nonwitch community for the encouragement and support that have helped me manifest my visions.

Thank you to the team at REDFeather Mind, Body, Spirit and Schiffer Publishing—Peter Schiffer, Chris McClure, Dinah Roseberry, Brenda McCallum, and Amy Fisher—for their incredible support. Thank you to Erika Robinson for offering valuable insights in the foreword and in our community.

A special thank-you to Ruth Ann and Wald Amberstone, the founders of the Readers Studio in New York City. Their invitation into the Tarot community with open arms and kindness afforded me the opportunity to meet and become friends with an incredible network.

CONTENTS

FOREWORD

ften, in ways simultaneously loving and belittling, Lenormand is referred to as "Tarot's Little Sister." As a longtime Lenormand reader, as a lover of language's lyricism, I think this is grounded in misunderstanding. Lenormand is a word language, which is entirely different from the language of Tarot. It must be learned as separately from Tarot as French must be from Chinese. To learn the rules of each one properly is an aid to appreciation. Lenormand is my primary instrument. I think of it more as an instrument than a tool, because of the music its language makes with practice, especially when in tune.

When we are small, we learn the meanings of discrete words: *dog, house,* and *tree.* We feel delight at being able to link black marks on a white page to an image we create in our minds, of a dog or a house or a tree. And thus we think we have learned to read, but we have barely begun. Lenormand moves us backward from this: from a picture to a word instead. We make that backward connection and think we can now read Lenormand. Again, we have just begun.

An individual word or Lenormand card can only tell us so much. We must learn to string them together. We start out doing so haltingly, as we did in primary school, as in "See Spot run." But practice begets poets from beginners, and *Shadowland Lenormand* is the perfect tool to show us why. In this deck, the Lenormand objects come alive, interact with, and are accompanied by whimsical characters who remind us that the ancestors are ever with us through all our trials and joys. These characters feel like stand-ins for ourselves, so the experience of reading with this deck feels quite like virtual reality: rich and satisfying, and instructive. With this deck, we can be fluent, fluid Lenormand readers, both for others and for ourselves.

As a Lenormandist, I often talk about being "in the company of the cards." I first discovered Lenormand as a new widow many years ago, and in my own pandemic time of isolation, which is what the state of widowhood first feels like. Lenormand was my one steadfast, reliable friend who solaced and steadied and steered. The *Shadowland Lenormand,* had it existed back then, might have shown me sooner the power of Lenormand to do this. It is a deck that beckons one inside oneself, to explore even the scary parts in safety.

—Erika Robinson

Erika Robinson, an English teacher and college admissions consultant for 30 years, has been reading Lenormand professionally for the past 15 years. Having received a degree in English and an MDiv degree from Harvard University, she has always been fascinated with language, and reads Lenormand with a unique style that brings her sitters awareness, insight, and comfort.

INTRODUCTION

Nightfall and darkness are often associated with danger. Fear of what we cannot see is a vestige of our ancestral memories of hungry beasts ready to pounce from the shadows.

Now we have spaces that keep us physically safe, relative to our ancestry, but what about psychological shadows? Swiss psychologist Carl Jung spent many years delving into the minds of patients and created a system of universal archetypes and symbols, synchronicity, and the collective unconscious. Raised by a religious father, and a mother who claimed to have spiritual visitations each night, perhaps this is why his theories and view of the universe are more open to spiritual possibilities than many mainstream psychological concepts.

Jung is also known for his theory that states we all have parts of our personalities rejected by our conscious ego due to embarrassment or fear. He named those lost, unrecognized parts of self as *shadows*. This is a complex issue, and while an oracle deck can't be considered a substitute for therapy, using this tool of self-awareness can offer suggestions for reflection and recognition, helping you integrate all parts of your personality.

In increasing self-awareness, we have the opportunity to become self-actualized and whole. We learn to accept that all human beings are imperfect, and perhaps then we can become kinder to ourselves as well as others. When we look into the shadows of our minds, we are not finding fault, criticizing, or beating ourselves up, but merely separating our internal issues from external ones, which will help us define our boundaries.

In my own witchcraft practice, I find comfort in the unknowable shadows that represent the liminal spaces of dusk, dawn, and nighttime. The magic of shadows and tools for divination represent spiritual portals into which I can travel and return with information. Let this deck be a tool for your self-awareness and growth, offering a way to travel to other realms to receive information.

Lenormand Cards

Lenormand cards provide an opportunity to communicate with spirits, ancestors, and our unconscious through symbols and methodologies designed to offer insights. To engage in shadow work as a path to reintegration and to access the spiritual realm, I have created the *Shadowland Lenormand*, which can be used by anyone at any level of experience.

In addition to understanding the basic history and language of the cards, I feel a divination system needs to share its symbolism in a way that prompts active reflection on the part of a reader or client. Using symbolism offers an accessible way of communicating because they transcend the barriers that written languages often create by taking abstract ideas and giving them form.

First appearing as the black-and-white House of Shadows Lenormand, this version has been redrawn, inked, and painted, with an expanded and updated booklet that includes a series of "Reflection Questions" for each card.

The art, aside from its color, is different from standard Lenormand cards because no single card is seen as strictly positive, negative, or neutral. While they can still be read in this way, the additional context offered in the art allows for more flexibility and freedom while reading.

The Petit Lenormand oracle deck symbols were generally thought of as originating from a German card game called the *Game of Hope* by Johannes Hechtel in 1799. The *Game of Hope* was a racing game in which cards were placed on a table and gaming pieces were used to move from card to card, depending on the numbers appearing with the roll of the dice. If a player landed on a positive card, a number of moves forward were granted; with a neutral card, no moves were gained; and with a negative card, there was a subsequent retreat. While some of the game's usage may have migrated to the Lenormand oracle, according to Tarot and oracle scholar Mary K. Greer, its symbols were likely an inspiration from coffee-ground reading symbolism originating in Turkey.

Marie Anne Lenormand, after whom the cards are named, was born in Alençon, Normandy, in 1772. At the age of five, she was sent to an orphanage, and according to popular lore, she was highly intuitive. As a teenager, she moved to Paris and soon became a well-known cartomancer, seer, and prolific author. At that time, Paris was ruled by General Napoléon, whose wife Josephine employed Madame Lenormand as a regular advisor. Mme. Lenormand maintained a reputation for accuracy throughout her life and was adept at reading with cards, also using astrology, palmistry, and several occult methods for offering advice.

Devoting her life to fortune-telling and writing, when she passed at the age of 71, her nephew and only living heir was apparently so convinced that his aunt had committed heresy that he burned all of her belongings and cards, except a few. Lore would suggest that two of the decks spared were what we now call the 52-card Grand Lenormand and the 36-card Petit Lenormand.

The Language of Lenormand

Lenormand cards are straightforward and provide a no-nonsense language and resource for diviners and those who use them for reflection. The simple language of 18th-century European, archetypal symbols can help us build sentences based on each word or words associated with each card. The sequence of the cards changes the meaning when read from left to right, and if you choose to follow this method, you need to understand the subtle differences.

For example, if I pull the Heart, Cross, and Coffin cards, I might read this as "Your heart is burdened by grief over the loss of someone, but you are in the process of beginning again." If, however, the cards were drawn in the sequence of Coffin, Heart, and Cross, I would say, "The ending of someone or something you thought could be resurrected is a heavy burden that is causing you heartache." The difference between beginning and ending with certain cards, or their sequence in general, can change the meaning of your interpretation, both subtly and dramatically.

The traditional Lenormand method of reading by proximity offers the ability to use positive, negative, and neutral cards in combinations that permit a broad range of interpretations and in this way offers a unique system quite different from traditional Tarot. You can use these cards for daily, single-card draws, as well as with many other spreads, as detailed in the "Cards Layout" section. Here I also share a quick overview of the full deck or grand tableau method of reading Lenormand cards.

The card descriptions that follow include a section on each card's "Shadow," which is an aspect of the card you may not normally see, whether you perceive it as welcome or not. For example, the Fox card meaning was quite stringent in the original Lenormand system, indicating deception. In my drawing, the fox is posing as a chicken, which still supports the traditional interpretation of the classic Lenormand system; however, in the accompanying "Reflection Questions" for this card, you will find shadows lurking in such questions as "Are you deceiving someone?" or "Are you the fox, the chicken, or the person holding the chicken?"

I wish you all the best in exploring the shadows, however you define them, and wish you insights that help you become and stay empowered. Enjoy!

THE CARDS

❶ RIDER

A little creature with antennae rides and waves from the top of a speedy, eight-legged creature.

KEY WORDS

Message, messenger, communication, speed, delivery, new romance, passion.

SHADOW

Fleeting, impulsive, reckless thoughts, words, or actions.

MESSAGE

Take notice—something or someone is arriving quickly and may be a simple letter or a new and exciting love interest. While we value speed, remember that it can sometimes lead to mistakes, especially if decisions are made impulsively. Scrutinize people or messages that seem too good to be true or those who pressure you into questionable commitments with fast-talk. There may be a quirky message or unusual delivery method attached to this message. The closer the Rider card is to the center of your spread or your chosen seeker (or significator card), the quicker the news; also, note the surrounding cards indicate the type of news. The card is a speed modifier and can evoke the word "fast" when interpreted in conjunction with other cards.

REFLECTION QUESTIONS

1. What type of news would make you happy at this moment?

2. Is there a particular romantic adventure that sounds intriguing to you?

3. Where or when do you act impulsively?

2

CLOVER

A four-leafed clover creature holds the hand of a young woman and a sack of coins.

KEY WORDS

Luck, fortune, opportunities, prosperity, wealth, relationships.

SHADOW

Gambling, ignoring a romantic connection, throwing money away, relying on luck instead of taking action.

MESSAGE

While this card denotes luck and prosperity in general, especially when this is the subject of the question being asked, it can also mean a short-lived turn of events. This may be a symbolic reminder not to sit back and wait for luck when action is required to achieve your goals. A card of light-heartedness and fun, it indicates playfulness and joy. Depending on the situation or context, it can also be a message to lighten up and enjoy life a little—you are lucky! In a reading with several cards, the Clover lessens difficult situations indicated by surrounding cards such as the Coffin or Scythe. If near the Garden, Heart, or Bouquet, luck in love is indicated.

REFLECTION QUESTIONS

1. What is in your control and out of control in your life right now?

2. Do you feel compelled to gamble as a result of relying on luck?

3. Where in your life could you be more playful or spontaneous?

3
SHIP

A ship is on a sea voyage with a large jellyfish lurking beneath.

KEY WORDS
Travel, business, merchants, visiting relatives in distant countries.

SHADOW
Mourning, loss or homesickness, hidden dangers.

MESSAGE
The ship is a symbol of business, journeys, and sometimes loss. The jellyfish is a cautionary reminder of what lays beneath the surface.

Generally a favorable card indicating business opportunities, but there may be hidden dangers. Remember to scrutinize the fine print on any contracts or agreements at this time. This may be a time to look deeply into grief or mourning that you may hide from yourself and others, or your fear of vulnerability. Note the sequence of cards in which your Ship appears so that you may understand whether the situation is arriving or departing. Also, look to surrounding cards such as the Scythe, which may indicate a sudden end to grieving, travel, or a business opportunity.

REFLECTION QUESTIONS

1. What journey are you delaying?

2. Do hidden fears stop you from moving forward in general?

3. What deep or underlying grief do you need to acknowledge?

4

HOUSE

*An active house
is filled with
many creatures and
one occupant
peering out from
behind.*

KEY WORDS

Home, dwelling, psyche, household activity,
neighborhood, neighbors, immediate family.

SHADOW

Too much activity in the home, entrapment,
psychological trauma or anxiety.

MESSAGE

This card indicates your physical home, your
neighborhood, and can be a metaphor for

your psyche as well. A lot of activity is indicated by the imagery, but not all of it may be welcome. Examine your relationship to your home environment for hidden fears, tensions, or stressors. Perhaps this is a time to look into the shadows to see if you are at peace with yourself, before assessing others in your home or neighborhood. Look at surrounding cards to see if there are additional issues in your immediate environment that are affecting your home life.

REFLECTION QUESTIONS

1. What steps could you take to make your home a sanctuary?

2. How might identifying any toxic attributes of your environment assist you?

3. How do you relate to your neighbors and neighborhood?

5
TREE

A person sits on a swing attached to a tree with adorned branches.

KEY WORDS
Health, well-being, lungs, heart, circulatory system, family, heritage, roots.

SHADOW
Ignoring health issues, especially circulatory or respiratory, being cut off from family, feeling physically ill.

MESSAGE
Life is a string of cumulative, personal experiences, as well as those passed down through

the generations. Look at your emotional, physical, spiritual, and psychological history. Examine your overall health and all influences. Remember that roots, while not always apparent, are at work as much as your branches or current experiences in supporting your feelings of safety and security. This card is asking you to look at everything you require for your overall well-being. It can indicate your extended family as well. Always note surrounding cards for more information and remember to check your health. Take special note if this appears next to the Coffin or Scythe, and ensure your lungs, heart, and circulatory systems are doing well.

REFLECTION QUESTIONS

1. How do you generally assess your overall well-being?

2. Do you have what you require right now to feel secure?

3. How often do you get physical checkups?

6

CLOUDS

*Several grumpy
clouds hover above
a young woman
with an umbrella.*

KEY WORDS

Temporary confusion, anxiety, bad mood, lack
of clarity, protection from a storm.

SHADOW

Long-term depression, anxiety, pessimism.

MESSAGE

The card is suggesting you may feel confused
or unable to see a situation clearly; it may also
indicate anxiety or a desire to hide from a

difficult circumstance, rather than identify and work with it. Clouds can create indecision or a cyncial outlook, but an umbrella can help. The umbrella is symbolic of something that will help protect you in case it rains. The umbrella also represents someone who is objective about your dilemma and is willing to offer advice. Don't hesitate to seek professional services if you can't see your way out of the storm. Remember that weather changes and the clouds will clear. Look to cards that are close by to see a specific area of anxiety or confusion and solutions.

REFLECTION QUESTIONS

1. What makes you feel pessimistic?

2. Do rainy days ever bring comfort to you?

3. What or who is your symbolic "umbrella" when stressed or confused?

7
SNAKE

*A large snake
sits coiled behind
a person who is
sitting on a bench
reading.*

KEY WORDS

Hidden, betrayal, gossip against you,
competitor, jealousy, behind your back.

SHADOW

Gossiping, betraying others, your own
jealousy and competitiveness.

MESSAGE

Think about competition at your workplace
or in your social circles. Do you know someone

who is clearly jealous of you or wants your job? See the situation for what it is. This can refer to self-sabotage as well as gossip from a colleague. Ignoring it may be detrimental if you are caught off guard; however, seeing it and refusing to be intimidated can also be an effective strategy. Check surrounding cards to see what action, if any, is indicated. A heightened awareness of your surroundings and particularly your work environment is suggested.

REFLECTION QUESTIONS

1. When have you felt betrayed?

2. Do you place your trust in people easily?

3. Looking at the card, would you advise the person on the bench to acknowledge the snake or ignore it?

8
COFFIN

A young alchemist raises a hand while reciting an incantation to raise the dead.

KEY WORDS
Ending and resurrection, completion and rebuilding, healing from sorrow.

SHADOW
Defeat, inability to begin again and move forward, refusal to acknowledge pain from loss.

MESSAGE
Death can be final in a physical sense, but, symbolically, we can resurrect the forgotten

desires, hopes, and dreams that have been locked away. This card can indicate the threat of, or, an actual job loss, refer to a relationship that has ended or is about to end, or loss in your family, depending on the question and surrounding cards. Remember, it is never too late to start again. However, the card also offers a cautionary note about trying to continue with something that is no longer viable. Do not waste your energy. Also, if you have misplaced an object, check for it in a box.

REFLECTION QUESTIONS

1. What should you be ending that no longer gives you joy?

2. Have you locked away grief that could be revisited and resolved?

3. What could you resurrect in your life that you thought was finished?

BOUQUET

A flower bouquet is offered from a shadowy figure.

KEY WORDS

Gift, ceremony, grace, charm, romance, appealing offer, proposition, charisma.

SHADOW

Strings attached to gifts, potential stalker, unwanted attention.

MESSAGE

A lovely offer is coming your way. Accept it with grace. It may be a proposal for a job, a gift from a romantic person, or simply a friend who appreciates you and is bringing a gift. The Bouquet references formal occasions, and ceremonial gifts, as well. Perhaps you are receiving a certificate of appreciation. While gifts are generally lovely things, consider the origin of the bouquet to see if there are any strings attached and check in with how you are feeling to ensure you are not receiving unwanted attention.

REFLECTION QUESTIONS

1. Do you prefer giving or receiving gifts?

2. What is an ideal romance for you?

3. Have you ever felt manipulated when receiving gifts or offered them to get your way?

10
SCYTHE

A reaper figure holds an ancient harvest tool known as a scythe.

KEY WORDS

Harvest, completion, unexpected or swift ending.

SHADOW

Sudden or continued aggression, potential violence.

MESSAGE

The Scythe can indicate an ending to a specific time period, a particular lifestyle, or a certain relationship. You may experience an abrupt or unexpected ending that may feel harsh. This card often shows up in a reading as a job or monetary loss if near finance or business cards such as the Fish, Moon, Clover, Star, or Ship. Sometimes the card is a warning of aggression, a sharp tongue, verbal abuse, or physical threats. Don't underestimate something that seems harmless but feels wrong. The card suggests you remove yourself from any unsafe situations that are not for your highest good or that do not ensure your complete well-being.

REFLECTION QUESTIONS

1. What sudden ending has left you residual insecurities?

2. Does fear of poor outcomes hold you back?

3. Have you assessed any relationships that feel abusive?

11
BROOMS

A witch and her cat hold brooms to clear away debris.

KEY WORDS

Cleaning, sweeping out unwanted energies, decluttering, boundaries, banishing.

SHADOW

Poor boundaries, clearing out the positive with the negative, imposing your energies onto others, hoarding.

MESSAGE

Time to clear out your environment and rid yourself of everything that is clutter in your life. You may be perceived harshly for it, but defining clear boundaries in all of your relationships may be more important to your overall health than whether you are perceived as nice. People, objects, and self-defeating thoughts or behaviors need to be swept away to make room for fresh and healthier ways of being. Remember to use your discretion and not to accidentally clear out the good with the bad.

REFLECTION QUESTIONS

1. What physical areas need clearing in your life?

2. What behaviors no longer serve your psychological needs?

3. Are there relationships in your life that need to be reevaluated?

⑫
BIRDS

A large bird holds a small person captive while two smaller birds look on.

KEY WORDS
Travel, busywork, juggling many small tasks, distractions.

SHADOW
Anxiety, chatting, gossip, feeling held captive by responsibilities.

MESSAGE
Sometimes we underestimate the impact of the nervous energy we expend on filling our

days with repetitive and multiple small activities. Anxieties can arise from everyday things we encounter such as bills, chores, errands, and the feeling of having to put out fires constantly to keep up. Try not to be held captive by perceived obligations. Birds may also mean several small trips, as well as gossip that distracts you from the important tasks you need to complete.

REFLECTION QUESTIONS

1. Are you jumping from one project to another without finishing any of them?

2. In what areas of your life do you desire freedom?

3. Does sharing gossip ever make you feel empowered?

CHILD

A young child holds a string connected to her head, like a balloon.

KEY WORDS

Esteem, valued, precious, innocence, imagination.

SHADOW

Immature, inexperienced, unrealistic, naïve, feeling inept.

MESSAGE

Cherished for their innocence and honesty, children are also be respected for their ability to surpass any adult's imagination. Because of their playful attitude and unique perspective, they can find creative and beautiful solutions beyond the usual adult-mind limitations. Perhaps looking at things from a child's point of view is suggested. Some may describe your behavior as "childish," meaning immature, but it's important to remember to hold on to the wonder and innocence of childhood. The modifier "small" is often used when this card appears next to other cards. For example, next to the Ship, it may mean a small or short trip or small business opportunity. This card may also indicate pregnancy or an actual child, depending on the question and context.

REFLECTION QUESTIONS

1. What do you miss most about being a child?

2. Were you or your behavior ever called "childish"?

3. What was your favorite pastime as a child?

14
FOX

A fox wears a chicken mask and sits beside a young person who is holding a chicken.

KEY WORDS

Camouflage, charming, strategic, well spoken, ability to be visible or invisible at will.

SHADOW

Deceit, jealousy, cunning, duplicity, dishonesty.

MESSAGE

Foxes, though good-looking animals, are cunning. Foxes are not always deceptive, but you must recognize them for what they are, regardless of what they present. This card often indicates fraud and deceit, and it can also be used as the modifier "wrong" in spreads. For example, Fox + Stork may mean the wrong time or place to move or begin a project. It can also indicate your ability to be strategic in a situation that may refer to a work-related rivalry or self-deception. The difference between the Fox and Snake cards is that the Snake represents an often hidden threat but the Fox appears as a person who uses charm as a mask to hide true intentions.

REFLECTION QUESTIONS

1. Where are you being deceitful in your life?

2. How do you deal with jealousy in yourself and others?

3. Are you charmed or deceived easily?

15
BEAR

A tiny figure stands on top of a sleeping bear surrounded by human bones.

KEY WORDS

Strong willed, powerful, mother or mother-in-law figure, finances, protective.

SHADOW

Troubles, strife, investment issues, threat, domineering behavior.

MESSAGE

The Bear can represent a mature person, often a mother figure who is strong and protective, or someone who can be overbearing and offer unsolicited advice. This card may also refer to a mentor or any mature person offering direction and advice. Sometimes when this card appears with other cards such as the Mountain card, it may refer to an impasse or a person who is blocking your passage. For some, expressing power is dangerous and can leave them frozen in anxiety and unable to express fears or vulnerabilities. At other times, strength may turn into inflexibility and unwillingness to compromise. Use your power wisely.

REFLECTION QUESTIONS

1. When you look at the drawing, do you identify with the figure standing on the bear, or the bear?

2. In which instance has your strength been an asset, a challenge, or unrecognized?

3. Do you have strong female role models in your life?

16
STAR

A young person sits high up in the sky on a star overlooking a cityscape.

KEY WORDS
Community, the internet, networking, success, optimism.

SHADOW
Isolation, arrogance, self-centeredness, overconfidence, being a loner.

MESSAGE
Sitting on a star offers great perspective and indicates that you are part of the bigger

picture. You are lucky, happy, and positive, with strong connections. Although most decks have many stars, I have only drawn one as a reminder that each community begins with one person who has a spark of an idea. We can use our optimism and connections to create a network that offers space to those who may feel left out. Ask yourself if you are connecting with everyone in your community. Remember a strong network is important for everyone's well-being.

REFLECTION QUESTIONS

1. Who is in your network?

2. How do you share information or support others in your community?

3. Which connections have you neglected?

17

STORK

A large, boot-wearing stork holds a person with a suitcase firmly in its beak.

KEY WORDS

Beginnings, a baby, a new project, new home, new work location, change.

SHADOW

Unwilling to begin a new project or move location, fear of change.

MESSAGE

If the Stork has shown up in your spread, it is reminding you that routine can easily transform into apathy. Perhaps it's time to pick up and move to a new job, home, or relationship, or even ... have a baby! This is a card of change, whether in the home, your work, or your perception of life in general. Perhaps travel plans or a promotion are on the horizon? Despite the general fear we all share when facing the unknown, this move is a positive step toward your new life.

REFLECTION QUESTIONS

1. How do you feel about moving to a new home?

2. What are you giving birth to at this moment?

3. What type of excitement do you crave?

18
DOG

A large flea wears a dog mask and is on a leash held by a companion.

KEY WORDS

Loyalty, friendships, trust, reliability, good partnerships.

SHADOW

Blind loyalty, accepting deceit, mistrust, lack of loyalty.

MESSAGE

Dogs represent friends and relationships considered loyal, but sometimes we only see them the way we want to and don't examine the relationship too closely, for fear of what lies beneath. This card is urging you to see your friends for who they really are, and evaluate what healthy boundaries are for you. Perhaps they are not as loyal as you think; then again, maybe a large flea makes for a good companion. This card can indicate a work ally or someone you are unaware of who is supporting you.

REFLECTION QUESTIONS

1. Where are you placing your loyalty right now?

2. How do you define trust?

3. Who do you consider your allies?

TOWER

A tiny figure stands at the top of a tower watching a floating phantom.

KEY WORDS

Strength, success, accountability, leadership, longevity, ethical authority.

SHADOW

Abuse of power, isolation, ego, fear of responsibility, bad boss.

MESSAGE

Sometimes being at the top of a tower offers a great vantage point, but if you are too afraid of responsibility, it can be a lonely space. If you are the boss, maybe you should get down to the cafeteria a bit more frequently and meet with workers. This card can also indicate leadership skills and being asked to use your authority in an ethical way. Longevity is indicated, as well as upcoming business in buildings such as courthouses, city hall, or institutions in general.

REFLECTION QUESTIONS

1. How do you feel about being a leader?

2. Does isolation factor into your fears of success?

3. What role models do you have for effective leadership?

20
GARDEN

Several unique characters gather together in a garden to socialize.

KEY WORDS

Friends, social gatherings, shared green spaces, community groups.

SHADOW

Social anxiety, introvert, needing excessive attention and validation.

MESSAGE

Whether a party in the garden or a space to meet new coworkers, this card indicates a gathering of people both in a professional or personal capacity. Often, we socialize or gather in public gardens, and—you never know—you may meet some very unique people shortly. The garden can also indicate convalescence or a much-needed break from an illness or new friendships and alliances. This card suggests one of your strengths is your community involvement and signifies an improvement in social status.

REFLECTION QUESTIONS

1. How do you feel about socializing in general?

2. Do you give yourself adequate time to recover from illness or stress?

3. How do you define *community*?

21

MOUNTAIN

*A small figure on
a path approaches
a mountain range
with an opening that
resembles a large
mouth with teeth.*

KEY WORDS
Large task, long journey, challenging situation.

SHADOW
Blockage, impasse, feeling defeated by challenges, insurmountable obstacles.

MESSAGE
A blockage may appear directly between you and your goal that causes concern or stops you from moving forward. Remember to

strategize, assess the situation carefully, and then proceed. Any blockage can be a challenge, whether related to one's health, professional life, personal relationships, or financial situation. You may have a symbolic mountain to overcome, but you don't necessarily need to climb to get to the other side. Taking one task at a time to feel less overwhelmed is advised. This may also be an opportunity to pause and rest before continuing, due to an impasse beyond your control.

REFLECTION QUESTIONS

1. How do you react to large issues or tasks?

2. When faced with obstacles, at what point do you feel like giving up, and when do you move ahead?

3. What alternative approaches could you consider?

22
CROSSROADS

*A devil holding
a pitchfork stands
at the center
of two intersecting
roads.*

KEY WORDS
Decision, change of direction, choice, crises, intersection.

SHADOW
Indecision, fear of change, immobility, lack of accountability.

MESSAGE
When you aren't sure which way to go, take a moment to pause and decide which direction is best. Though you may receive a tempting

offer while deciding which direction to take, trust your gut and remain calm. Assess your goals and situation carefully to choose wisely, but choose—you don't want to linger at the crossroads for very long. Remaining stuck in long-term indecisiveness can cause undue stress and deteriorate your quality of life. Often the crucial message here is to make a choice, not what your ultimate choice may be. You can always change your mind. Look at surrounding cards for a clue as to which direction to choose.

REFLECTION QUESTIONS

1. When faced with decisions how do you react?

2. Which choices have been easiest to make and which ones have been the most difficult?

3. When you travel do you use visual cues for direction, a GPS, or both?

23
MICE

A two-headed mouse is eating an apple.

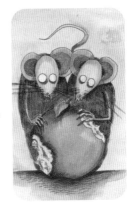

KEY WORDS
Petty theft, small worries, incremental losses, deterioration.

SHADOW
Ignoring anxiety, addressing small issues without addressing the source, allowing ourselves to be slowly depleted.

MESSAGE
Keep an eye on your possessions and guard against theft or loss. Also indicates smaller

stresses you encounter that accumulate and take their toll on your health over time. Don't underestimate your part in some losses and remember to remain vigilant about cash or material loans at this time. Secure your home from pests or rodents, and keep an eye on your storage areas. Surrounding cards will shed light on the types of losses and anxieties you will experience. If close to the central or seeker (or significator) card, you may recover items; if far away from it, the loss is likely to be permanent.

REFLECTION QUESTIONS

1. List five small things that make you crazy.

2. What five things would you keep in your spiritual cupboard at all times?

3. What do mice represent to you?

24
HEART

A flying night spirit carries a heart that has been wounded and repaired many times.

KEY WORDS

Love, compassion, emotion, lasting relationships.

SHADOW

Ignoring grief and heartache, infatuation, fear of vulnerability.

MESSAGE

Love is important, but don't give your heart away or let someone steal it. We are much stronger than we feel, and our hearts have survived tremendous loss and sorrow. The scars are a testament to our resilience and experiences. Consider who you love right now, and make sure you let them know. Whether romantic or platonic, love and deep compassion are coming your way when you pull this card.

REFLECTION QUESTIONS

1. Do you hide the wounds in your heart?

2. When do you feel safe to share your heart's desire?

3. Where do you place most of your love and compassion?

RING

Two gender-neutral beings sit on top of a gemstone ring, symbolizing commitment.

KEY WORDS

Personal and business partnerships, pledge, teamwork, commitment, union, marriage.

SHADOW

Isolation, lack of commitment, ego, separation.

INTERPRETATION

When this card shows up near the central card or seeker (significator), you are going to experience a relationship commitment, but remember to think about what this means to you in the long term and look at your situation from a higher perspective. This card indicates partnerships and serious agreements, contracts, or commitments. Note any surrounding cards to indicate the type or context of the ring. If you asked for romantic advice, good timing for an upcoming marriage or engagement is indicated.

REFLECTION QUESTIONS

1. Do you long for partnership of some type?

2. Is this a time to ask for collaboration in business to share your workload?

3. How do you feel about romantic commitments in general?

26
BOOK

A person sits in a study reading a book, seeking relaxation and answers.

KEY WORDS

Knowledge, information, secret, studying, education, inquiry, wisdom.

SHADOW

Ignorance, gossip, misinformation, rumors, being dogmatic or rigid.

MESSAGE

This card speaks about information you are seeking or that may be shared with you. It can also indicate writing, research, academic papers, and studying for tests or exams. This may also be the time to write a book, short story, or journal your thoughts. You may need to review instructions or manuals. Perhaps it's time to quit work altogether and read books by your favorite author to unwind.

REFLECTION QUESTIONS

1. How willing are you to spend time reflecting and finding the answers you seek?

2. When does studying seem intimidating to you?

3. What type of knowledge provides you with self-confidence and security?

27
LETTER

A flying bat holds a letter in his claws.

KEY WORDS

Correspondence, text message, email, contract, written document, or communication.

SHADOW

Procrastination of correspondence, poor communication skills.

MESSAGE

Some written news is coming your way. Expect a bill, message, or email that may be business or personal. The bat symbolizes transformation and twilight, and may indicate spiritual news or news of upcoming changes that are unexpected or unconventional. You are also being asked to stay in touch or correspond with people you haven't spoken with in a while. Look to surrounding cards for specific information about the type of news arriving.

REFLECTION QUESTIONS

1. Are you up to date with sending correspondence?

2. What letter did you receive in the past that affected you deeply?

3. Have you ever misinterpreted a letter's meaning or intent? When did this occur?

28
MAN

A man with bat wings hovers above the ground.

KEY WORDS

This image represents a man or male-identified seeker in a reading.

SHADOW

Inability to see a person as a complex individual beyond their creed, age, gender, ethnicity, or abilities.

MESSAGE

This card can represent a male, a male-iden-tified person, or an archetype of masculinity who is either the subject in the reading or the love interest of the seeker. This "man" enjoys nighttime and navigates with or is especially sensitive to sound. Look to other cards to see the context of meeting, seeing, or interacting with this person, and pay close attention to distance within larger spreads. The farther away, the less impact this person will have on you. This card is also an indication of emotional distance. If it represents the seeker, look to surrounding cards for context.

REFLECTION QUESTIONS

1. When do you feel close to someone emotionally?

2. What are your male role models, if any?

3. What do you consider masculine traits?

29
WOMAN

An archetype of femininity is out walking her spider.

KEY WORDS

Symbolic femininity, a female gender identification, a female-identified love interest or person close to you.

SHADOW

Inability to see a person as a complex individual beyond their creed, age, gender, ethnicity, or abilities.

MESSAGE

This card represents a female-identified person or the partner or important person in relation to the seeker in a reading. Pets, loyalty, and companionship are very important to this person. If this card indicates the seeker, look to surrounding cards for context. This card may also indicate a female-identified boss or partner with whom you are going to reconnect with shortly.

REFLECTION QUESTIONS

1. How do you define femininity?

2. What constitutes loyalty to you?

3. What female role models do you have currently or have you had in the past?

LILY

An elderly person holds a lily while a cat sleeps on the floor.

KEY WORDS

Maturity, experience, platonic love, wisdom, happiness, loyalty.

SHADOW

Immaturity, imprudence, bitterness, lack of loyalty.

MESSAGE

This card represents a mature male- or a female-identified person who is experienced.

Wisdom comes with age and this card often represents a mentor or professor figure. The Lily indicates both sexual desire as well as platonic relations. It may indicate an older person with secret desires or one who reminisces a great deal about past romances. The card may also indicate loyal, older community members, or platonic family relationships with a "grandfatherly" or "fatherly" figure. The lily suggests a mature perspective and offers peace and happiness.

REFLECTION QUESTIONS

1. How does your overall experience relate to your personal relationships?

2. Do you currently have a mentor?

3. About what or whom do you reminisce?

31
SUN

A figure stands among trees, holding the sun tethered by a string.

KEY WORDS
Positive energy, warmth, optimism, summer, success, happiness, joy, carefree, outdoors.

SHADOW
Feeling pressure to be cheerful and smile, fear of success, inability to allow yourself time to be joyous and playful.

MESSAGE
This is a card of optimism and success. The Sun card brings joy and warmth, so enjoy your

day! Success can bring great responsibilities and requires careful consideration. Sometimes our accomplishments feel mysterious; try to understand how you achieved your goals so you have developed a methodology to repeat your process. This card also asks you to examine how you define success and to help you ignore the definitions of those who do not share your values and ethics. The surrounding cards may indicate the area in which you can expect joy or victory.

REFLECTION QUESTIONS

1. Do you act happy when you don't feel this way?

2. What is your idea of success, and how does it differ from those ideas of others?

3. What place offers you the greatest joy?

32
MOON

A small person clutches and dangles from the nose of a full moon's mask.

KEY WORDS
Career, fame, promotion, being well regarded in your profession.

SHADOW
Insecurity, inability to accept compliments, timidity.

MESSAGE
Fame may be knocking at your door, as your colleagues and community acknowledge your

skills. Your peers see you as accomplished in your profession. You will be recognized for your contributions, but remember that how we present ourselves publicly must be in line with who we truly are for our success to be authentic and lasting. If you have achieved a great deal of success, look carefully at the stresses you experience due to competition. Hang in there, and remember you worked hard to get where you are.

REFLECTION QUESTIONS

1. How do you feel your peers see your professional reputation?

2. When do you feel invisible in your career or job?

3. What personality differences do you feel you present publicly and privately?

KEY

*A flying
night spirit carries
a large key.*

KEY WORDS

Knowledge, access, responsibility, solution, opportunities, breakthrough, insight, epiphany.

SHADOW

Ignorance, inaccessibility, elitism, systemic prejudice, denying access, secrets.

MESSAGE

You will be given access to a space, knowledge, or perhaps a promotion, and this is a positive step. Look at who is offering you the key, and remember you don't need to accept. The key is a symbol of accessing both physical and symbolic spaces, often meaning knowledge, an epiphany, or sudden realization. The key shows up in spreads with symbols ahead or behind which specifically point to the "key" or solution to the question presented.

REFLECTION QUESTIONS

1. What knowledge are you seeking?

2. What things are inaccessible for you?

3. What realizations have occurred to you recently?

FISH

Three fish in business attire stand together waiting for a ride to a meeting.

KEY WORDS

Business opportunities, financial gain, money deals.

SHADOW

Lack of opportunity, financial losses, empty promises.

MESSAGE

Looks like good timing for a business deal of some sort! An offer, investment, or opportunity is coming your way through professional contacts. This is a positive card, signaling a good time to enter into contracts. If something seems fishy, don't sign on the dotted line. Determine the legitimacy of all agreements by getting advice from a professional. Don't be afraid to take what is being offered to you through your business connections.

REFLECTION QUESTIONS

1. What potential business opportunities do you feel you have?

2. How do you assess risk when entering into agreements?

3. What financial aspirations do you hold?

35
ANCHOR

An octopus holds on to an anchor at the bottom of the ocean.

KEY WORDS
Security, safety, hope, rest, stability.

SHADOW
Feeling stuck, inability to leave a seemingly secure situation, loss of hope.

MESSAGE
This card represents safety and all things that help us feel secure in our environment. It also represents hope. It may be time to stay home,

instead of traveling, and rest. If it's time to pick up your Anchor and go, you should! Examine what may have its tentacles on you, and then decide if oppression is masquerading as security, or if you genuinely feel comfortable where you are. This card can indicate your need to hold on to things that no longer provide you with what you need or may even hold others back.

REFLECTION QUESTIONS

1. Where is your safe haven?

2. What causes you to feel confined?

3. What gives you the greatest hope?

36
CROSS

A person in a mourning dress holds a large crucifix while a cat looks on.

KEY WORDS
Faith, allowing room for grief and loss, accepting responsibility.

SHADOW
Denying grief and loss, difficult times, feeling unnecessarily obliged.

MESSAGE
Grief and mourning can be a burden and may appear when we least expect it. During diffi-

cult moments, try to hold on to the understanding that everything is cyclic and changes—even if it does so slowly. While we each have a proverbial "cross to bear," try to remain grounded and calm by distinguishing between your wants and needs. The black cat in this drawing represents the side of us that says, "No big deal. It may look scary, but I got this." This card can also represent a spiritual person of any faith or gender identification.

REFLECTION QUESTIONS

1. What are your current obligations?

2. Where do you place your faith?

3. Have you denied yourself time to grieve?

HOW TO
USE THE CARDS

Timing

Ironic as this may sound, it is best to avoid seeking answers when you are very upset. Feeling stressed when you read will cloud your ability to be objective. I strongly advise everyone to wait until they feel calm enough to see the cards for what they are saying without projecting what you want or perhaps fear. Don't forget that an oracle deck is not a replacement for expert medical, financial, or legal advice. The cards offer advice and suggestions based on your current path. You are always free to change your path.

Effective Questions

Most seasoned readers will tell you that the key to receiving absolute clarity in any reading is not about the answer alone but the ability to ask effective questions. For example, if you choose a daily morning card ritual and ask the question "What do I need to know for today?" and you pull the Tree card, it makes sense to take a general view of the interpretation, such as "Watch your overall well-being." However, if you frame your question as "What area of my health should I have checked, if any?" and receive the Tree card, it is likely pointing to circulatory or respiratory areas. If you received the Heart card, then it would be wise to check your heart. If a financial card shows up in response to your health question then the Tree card is speaking about your financial health or the finances you use to support healthcare.

This applies if you are offering others readings as well. For example, clients who ask me whether they should or should not do something could be answered with a yes or no; however, most situations are not that simple. I offer the context and likely outcomes of a variety of possible choices so that a client can see their situation in terms of cause and effect, rather than judging an outcome as simply good or bad.

In my practice, using cards to "see" or spy on what others are thinking or doing is uncomfortable and unethical for me. If a client asks me where their "ex" is currently or if they will return, I keep the focus of the reading on the client and what they can do to move forward and how they can view the situation to gain objectivity and clarity and to heal.

Spiritual Hygiene and Reading Environment

I believe oracle cards are a spiritual portal to receive messages, and because of this, when I begin a reading, I use smoke or sprays to cleanse the space and call my ancestors for assistance with the lighting of my working candle. You can use any method or space you feel is free from distraction or negativity and, of course, call in (or not call in) whatever spiritual assistance you use in your own practice. When I am finished reading, I close the portal by thanking my ancestors, putting out the candle, and putting away my cards.

How to Shuffle

Handling the cards is the most important aspect of shuffling—not your methodology. One way is to place all cards facedown on a surface and mix them up, then collect them into one pile.

You can also shuffle cards as you would with any card game. Take your time, focus on the intent of what you are asking, and simply ensure you have mixed the order of the cards enough so that when you pull them from the deck, they are not in numerical sequence. If they are, simply put the cards back into the deck and continue to shuffle until they are well mixed.

How to Use Lenormand Cards with Other Divination Systems

I have been mixing and matching oracle cards and other divination methods for many years. As a young child, I would choose small beach pebbles to use as oracles, and as I matured, I added a variety of methods to my practice including many types of oracle cards, playing cards, curio casting, runes, and scrying.

Because Tarot was more familiar at the time I received my first Lenormand deck, as a teenager, I used the Tarot to support my understanding of Lenormand cards. Now I mix and match many different systems so that I can gain a wider perspective and variety of ways of seeing the situation.

Try crystals, rocks, oracles, curios such as metal coins or bones, or Tarot with Lenormand to expand your divination skills. I would advise that whichever systems you choose to combine, you use them respectfully by understanding their original usage, culture, and lore.

CARD LAYOUTS

Single-Card Reading

MORNING CARD AND EVENING REFLECTION

Leave time early in the morning to sit quietly with your deck and a journal.

Draw a single card, and record it with a few key points.

You can do this and meditate on the image, noting whatever comes to mind, or you may ask a specific question, such as "Which message do I need right now to help me with challenges or situations of the day?," writing down your answers, or using the reflection questions from the book.

Check back later in the evening to see what happened during the day that relates to the message you received. Sometimes the connections are apparent; other times they are subtle.

This is often effective if repeated over a series of days instead of simply once, so you can keep track of any changes, progressions, or patterns.

After you have made notations about your card or cards over a period of time, take a moment to reflect on the following:

1. What advice are you being given in general and specifically?
2. How did your message manifest or unfold throughout the day, week, or month?
3. Over a period of time, was this card or group of cards reflecting your current life, warning, or encouraging?

Two-Card Spread for Shadows

TWO-CARD SHADOW SPREAD

Shuffle and place one card facedown on the left and another to the right of it, also facedown. Turn over the first card, and take notes. Then turn over the second card, and consider its implications and suggestions. Reflect and journal about both of these cards, and remember to look at all aspects of both.

1. This is the shadow you are not recognizing.
2. This is the solution to or advice for your shadow.

Three-Card Spreads

ANCESTRAL INSPIRATION

I use this layout when faced with choices that are more intricate, and when I feel the need to call upon the strength of ancestors for clarity. I use the term *ancestors* to refer to family or community that stretches back to the dawn of our existence. If you wish to call upon a specific relative that you think may assist, it is best not to expect the person has suddenly become all-knowing or has great advice simply because they've died.

To begin, shuffle and lay three cards faceup, one at a time, from left to right.

1. The first card on the left signifies the cause of your situation.
2. The second from the left or middle card indicates your challenge.
3. The third card on the far right indicates the suggestion your ancestors are offering as a resolution to your situation.

MIND, BODY, AND SPIRIT—FOR SEEKING BALANCE

Shuffle and lay three cards faceup, one at a time, from left to right.

1. The first card on the left signifies your body and how your health is at the moment. Look at all of the advice contained within the card, as well as the physical outcome or comment.

2. The second and middle card indicates where your current state of mind is and any challenges you may be facing at the moment.
3. The third card on the far right indicates how your spiritual health is at the moment, and will offer suggestions or outlets for you to express your spirituality.

Nine-Card Blockbuster

This particular spread is perfect for facilitating breakthroughs, and offers clarity when you are engaging in creative problem solving and unsure of what is blocking your progress. Ensure you are building sentences or reading all three cards in context.

To create the layout:

Shuffle the cards well and clear your mind; then focus on the perceived problem you wish to resolve.

1. Place the first card facedown in front of you.
2. Card number two is then placed to the left and card number three to the right of card number one.
3. Cards number four, five, and six will be placed from left to right and directly below the first three cards.
4. Cards seven, eight, and nine are then drawn left to right and placed above the center row.

To interpret the layout:

1. Read the center row from left to right in a full sentence. This is the core issue of your block.
2. Read the bottom row from left to right as the series of incidences that contributed to your block or reinforce it. This is a deep shadow that remains hidden from your conscious mind.
3. The top row reading from left to right represents the solution and a higher perspective to your situation, so you can remove the block through action.

Le Grand Tableau

Le Grand Tableau, or the big view or picture, is the most famous Lenormand spread. It requires all 36 cards to be placed on the table at once, and cards are read by proximity and in relation to the seeker (or significator) card. There are so many different ways to read this spread, so I am offering my favorite methodology. I use this spread for general readings that require all aspects of a person's current situation, such as relationships, finances, career, and health, as well as for readings that address longer periods of time.

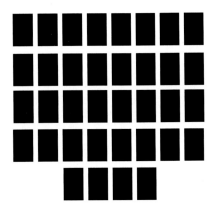

Shuffle the deck, and when you are ready, place a row of eight cards faceup from left to right. Then, place a second row of eight cards underneath. Continue with rows three and four. Place the last four cards centered, along the bottom.

If you wish to use the traditional method of using a seeker or significator card, locate the man or woman card and use it to represent you or the person for whom you are reading. Keep in mind you can use either gender and not be restricted to the heteronormative view of gender. If you feel drawn to another card, choose it before you place the cards. I just use the center card as the starting point and go from there without a significator. Try both ways to see which you prefer.

From the location of your chosen focal-point card, begin by reading the cards to the left in sequence and then to the right. Often we interpret cards to the left or preceding the seeker card as events in the past and those to the right as events coming up in the near future. All cards closest to the focal card or significator have the strongest impact, and the cards that are the farthest have the least impact.

I read the layout in relation to the position of the seeker card, including those above and below. The cards beneath your focal point are the subconscious or shadows you may not be recognizing, and the cards above reflect the higher self and things to consider as advice.

To find out about specific areas such as finances (Fish, Ship, Clover), relationships (Ring, Heart, Moon, Garden), and health (Heart, Tree), locate each card and then interpret the cards nearest to them, as well as their proximity to your seeker card. The final four cards along the bottom are what I refer to literally as the *bottom line,* or the summary of advice for your reading.

Lenormand with Other Divination Methods

If you feel stuck, find yourself in a rut, or feel you are reading the same messages repeatedly, try something different and think of what other divination systems you enjoy using, such as crystals, curios, or Tarot cards. Simply try asking a question, drawing a card, and then using a curio, rune, or crystal, and placing them together.

LENORMAND WITH TAROT

Try using a single card and asking a question. Place your Lenormand card upright in front of you. Shuffle your Tarot deck and pull a card, placing it upright next to your Lenormand card. Ask yourself the following:

1. What symbols, if any, are repeated?
2. How do these two images work together or contradict one another?

CONCLUSION

Remember that practice is required when using any system, so don't get discouraged if the meanings aren't always clear. Often it is our intuition that steps in to indicate what the cards are trying to tell us, as long as we approach with an open heart and mind.

I hope you enjoy this new, color version of my favorite *House of Shadows* characters, and if you wish to offer your insights, experiences, or to subscribe to the newletter, contact me through my website (https://www.monicabodirsky.com) or on social media @monicabodirsky on Instagram and IGTV, @monicabodirsky on Twitter, monicabodirskyshadowland on YouTube, and @monicabodirskydesign on FB.

For wholesale inquiries, please contact REDFeather Mind, Body, Spirit and Schiffer Publishing.

Happy Divining!
Monica

BIBLIOGRAPHY

Jung, C. G. (conceived and edited by). 1964. *Man and His Symbols*. New York: Anchor Books.

http://lenormanddictionary.blogspot.com/p/lenormand-suits.html

https://www.britannica.com/biography/Carl-Jung/Character-of-his-psychotherapy

https://www.britishmuseum.org/collection/term/BIOG182148

https://marykgreer.com/tag/lenormand/